D1541017

Editor    April McCroskie
Language Consultant    Professor Viv Edwards

**Dr Gerald Legg** holds a doctorate in zoology from Manchester University. His current position is biologist at the Booth Museum of Natural History in Brighton.

**Carolyn Scrace** is a graduate of Brighton College of Art, specialising in design and illustration. She has worked in animation, advertising and children's fiction. She is a major contributor to the popular *Worldwise* series.

**Professor Viv Edwards** is professor of Language in Education and director of the *Reading and Language Information Centre* at the University of Reading.

**David Salariya** was born in Dundee, Scotland, where he studied illustration and printmaking, concentrating on book design in his postgraduate year. He has designed and created many new series of children's books for publishers in the U.K. and overseas.

An SBC Book
Conceived, edited
and designed by
The Salariya Book Company
25 Marlborough Place Brighton BN1 1UB
© The Salariya Book Company Ltd MCMXCVII

First published in Great Britain by
Franklin Watts
96 Leonard Street
London
EC2A 4RH
First American edition 1998 by
Franklin Watts
A Division of Grolier Publishing
Sherman Turnpike
Danbury, CT 06816

The Cataloging-In-Publication Data is available from the Library of Congress

ISBN 0-531-14493-3

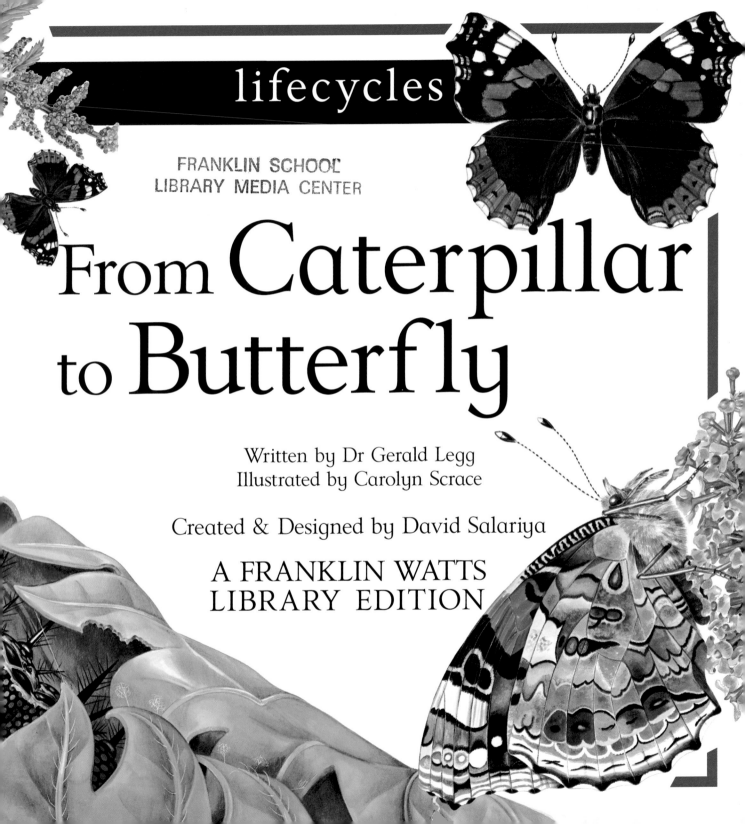

# lifecycles

# From Caterpillar to Butterfly

Written by Dr Gerald Legg
Illustrated by Carolyn Scrace

Created & Designed by David Salariya

A FRANKLIN WATTS
LIBRARY EDITION

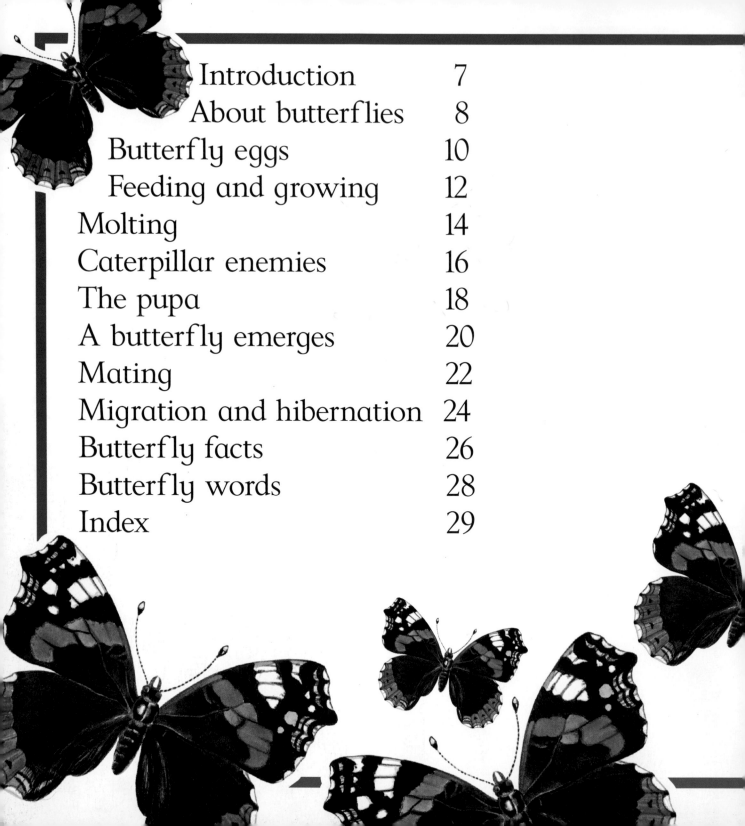

A butterfly starts life as an egg.
A caterpillar hatches from the egg.
The caterpillar grows and changes
into a pupa. A beautiful butterfly
hatches from the pupa. In this book
you can see
this amazing
life cycle
unfold.

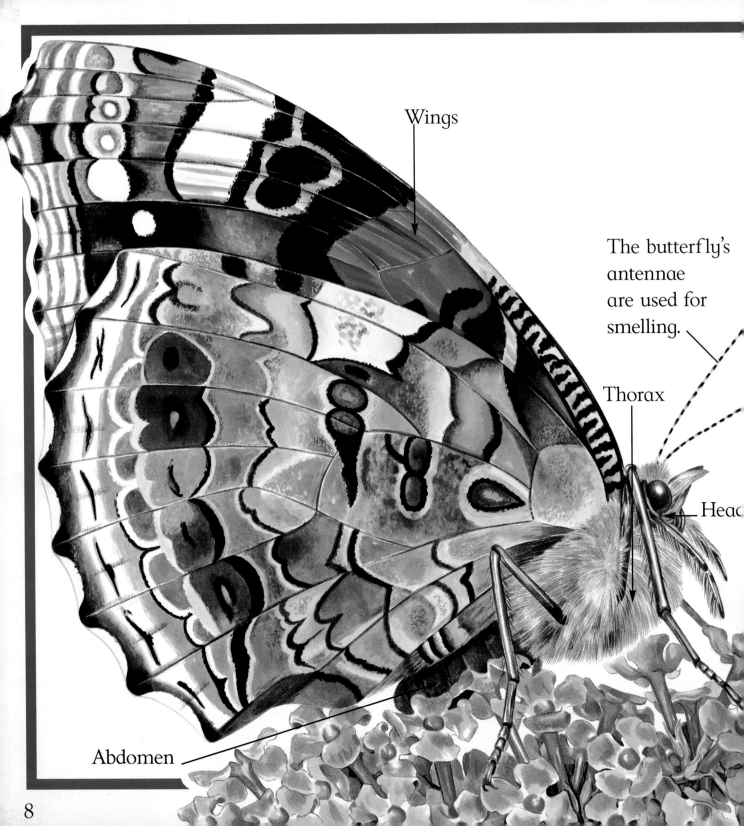

Wings

The butterfly's antennae are used for smelling.

Thorax

Head

Abdomen

8

The butterfly
is an insect.
This means its body
is in three parts.
The head is at the
front. The thorax
is in the middle.
The abdomen is
at the back.

The butterfly
uncoils its tongue
to suck up nectar.

Female butterflies
lay their eggs on leaves.
The eggs stick to the leaves
so the eggs will not fall off.
The baby insect grows
inside the sticky egg.
When it hatches
it is a caterpillar.

Leaf

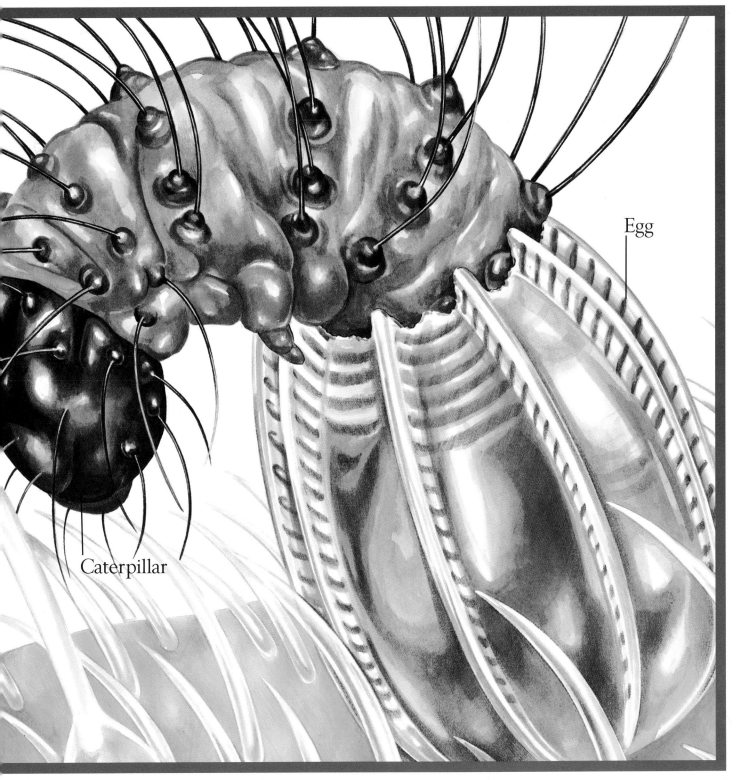

Egg

Caterpillar

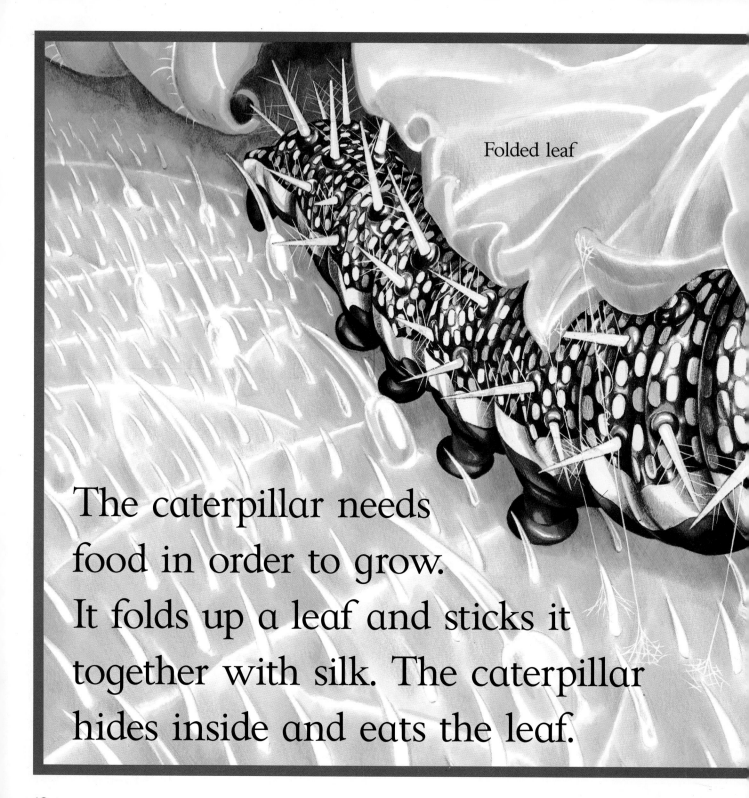

Folded leaf

The caterpillar needs
food in order to grow.
It folds up a leaf and sticks it
together with silk. The caterpillar
hides inside and eats the leaf.

Silk

Mouth

13

Caterpillar

Old skin

As the
caterpillar
grows,
it sheds its skin.
This is called molting.

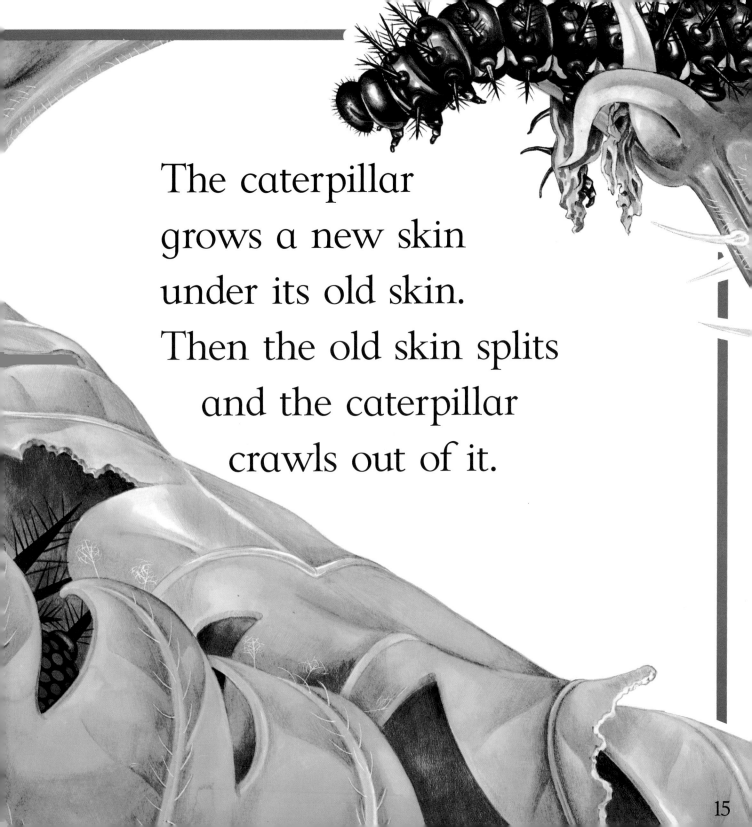

The caterpillar
grows a new skin
under its old skin.
Then the old skin splits
and the caterpillar
crawls out of it.

Bird

Many animals like
to eat caterpillars.
Caterpillars make a
juicy treat for spiders,
wasps, and birds.

Spider

Caterpillar

This caterpillar
is protecting itself
by hiding in a leaf.

Wasp

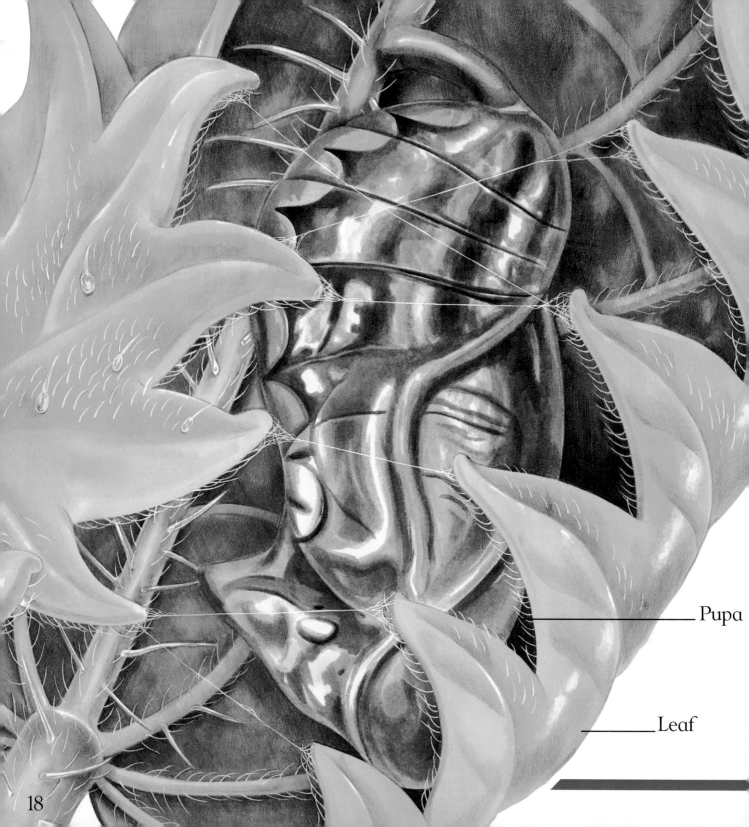

Pupa

Leaf

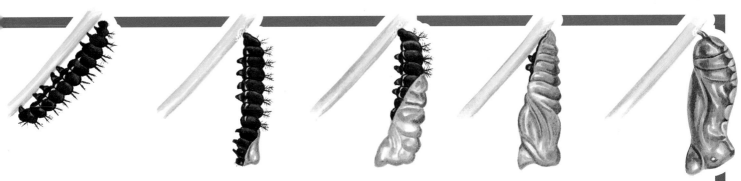

The fully grown caterpillar sits on a leaf stem.

The caterpillar hangs by a silk thread.

The caterpillar changes into a pupa.

It takes a few hours for the pupa to form.

The butterfly grows inside the pupa.

When the caterpillar is fully grown, it gets ready to turn into a butterfly. It hangs down on a silk thread from a leaf stem. Then it sheds its skin for the last time to form a pupa. Inside the pupa, the caterpillar changes into a butterfly.

After about three weeks
the pupa splits open.
The butterfly
crawls out.
Its new wings
are damp and wrinkled.
The butterfly climbs up
the plant and shakes out
its wings to dry them.
Then it flies away.

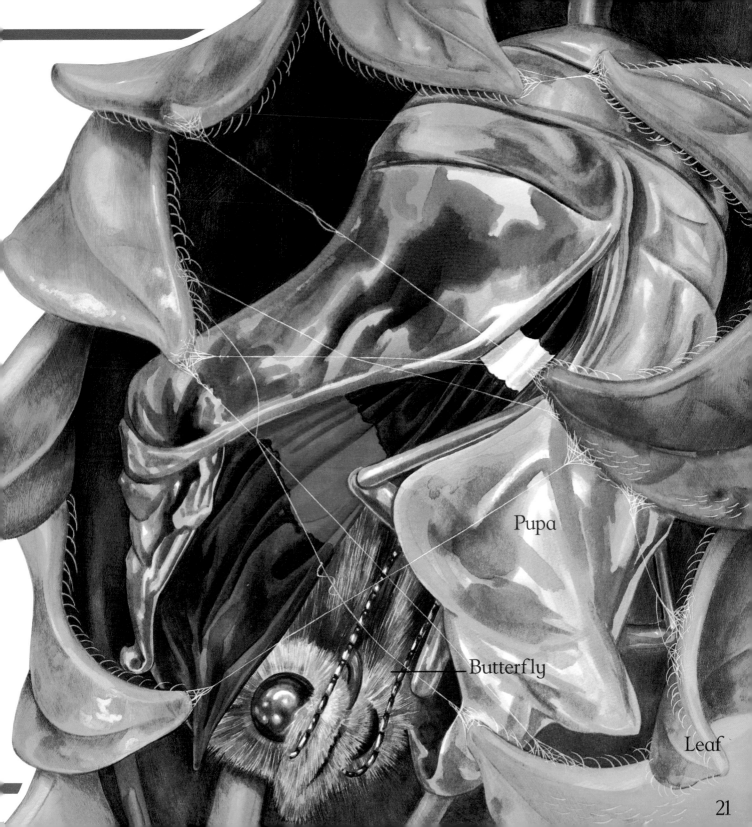

Pupa

Butterfly

Leaf

21

Male and female butterflies feed on the same flowers. Sometimes, they rest on a leaf to mate. The female butterfly then flies away to lay her eggs.

Leaf

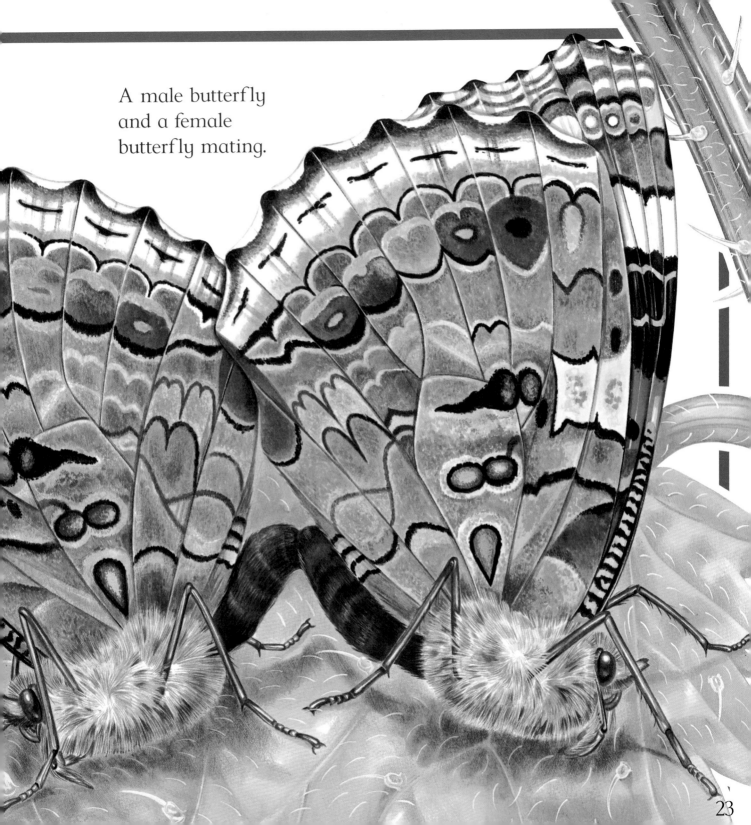

A male butterfly
and a female
butterfly mating.

23

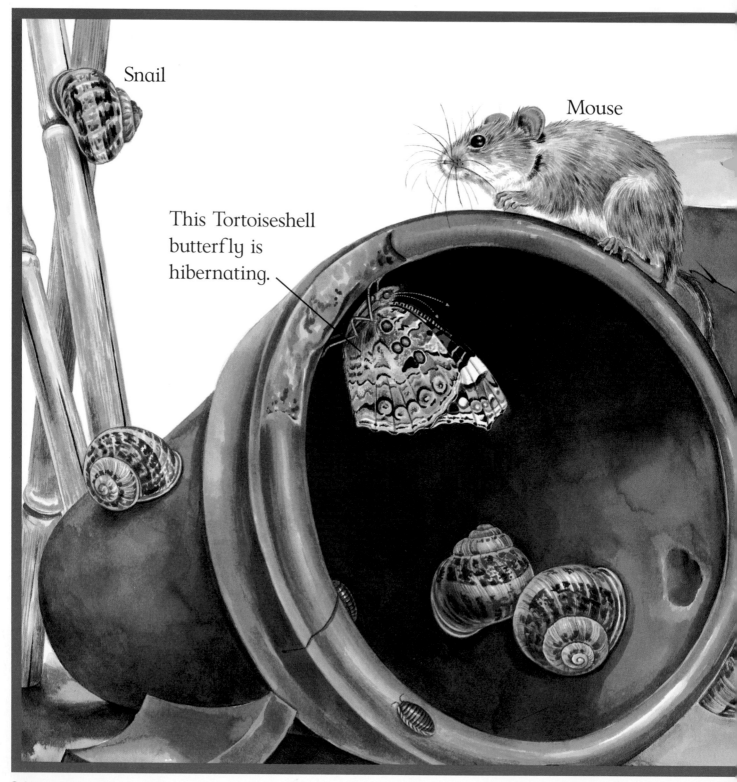

Snail

Mouse

This Tortoiseshell butterfly is hibernating.

24

Some butterflies fly thousands
of miles, across countries
and oceans, to lay their eggs
or find the right food.
This is called migration.
In winter butterflies look for
a warm, dry place to sleep.
This is called hibernation.

# Butterfly facts

A butterfly is an insect that flies during the day. It has antennae with club-shaped tips.

A moth is an insect that flies mainly at night. It has antennae that are thread-like or feathery.

The largest butterfly is the birdwing butterfly of New Guinea. It is 11 inches long.

The smallest butterfly is the dwarf blue butterfly of South Africa. It is just over 4 inches long.

The best flyer is the painted lady butterfly, which is found in most countries of the world. It can fly 620 miles without resting.

The fastest flyer is the monarch butterfly of North America. It can fly 20 miles per hour.

Monarch butterflies hibernate in groups of tens of thousands.

Butterflies beat their wings between 8 and 12 times a second.

Some butterflies only live for one day, but other butterflies can live for 4-5 months.

The owl butterfly of South America has markings on its wings that make it look like an owl. This helps to frighten its enemies.

The caterpillar of the Jamaican swallow-tail butterfly hides by pretending to be a bird-dropping. This way its enemies do not recognize that it is a tasty meal.

Zebra butterflies from the Americas are brightly colored. They do not bother to hide since they are poisonous and are left alone by their enemies.

The African leaf butterfly lies down among dead leaves to rest. Its wings look exactly like dead leaves, so its enemies do not see it.

The sixty-nine butterfly of South America looks like it has the number 69 on its wings.

Egg

Developing caterpillar

Pupa

Adult butterfly

## The growth of a butterfly

In the pictures above you can see how a butterfly grows from a tiny egg to a caterpillar then into a pupa and finally into a magnificent butterfly.

# Butterfly words

**Abdomen**
The rear part of an insect's body.

**Antennae**
The feelers on the head of an insect. Antennae are used for smelling.

**Caterpillar**
The stage in the life of a butterfly or moth just after it hatches from the egg.

**Hibernation**
When an animal sleeps through the winter.

**Insect**
An animal with a hard outer skin. An insect's body has 3 parts: a head, a thorax and an abdomen. Insects have 6 legs and 2 antennae.

**Mating**
The joining of a male (father) and a female (mother) to make babies.

**Migration**
When an animal travels a long way, at certain times of the year, to find a better place to live.

**Molting**
When an animal sheds its skin in order to grow.

**Nectar**
Sweet, sugary syrup made by flowers to attract insects.

**Pupa**
The stage in the life of a butterfly or moth between the caterpillar and the adult insect.

**Thorax**
The middle part of an insect's body.

# Index

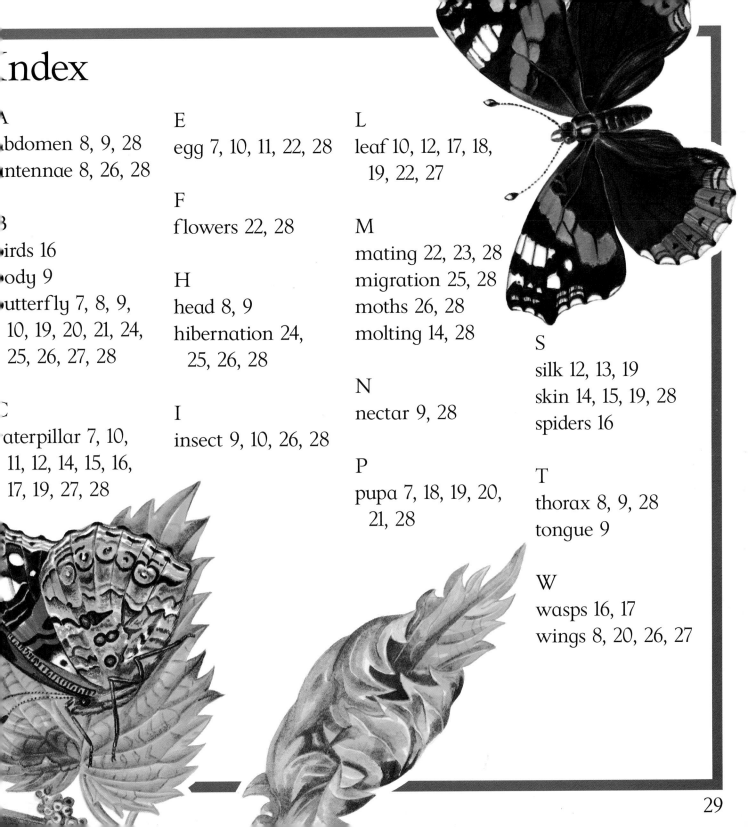

## DATE DUE

| | | | |
|---|---|---|---|
| | | | |
| | | | |
| | | | |
| | | | |
| | | | |
| | | | |
| | | | |
| | | | |
| | | | |
| | | | |
| | | | |